The STRAWBERRY Festival

by
Meaghan Fisher
art
Sandra Burns

Gypsy
Publications

Published in 2015, by Gypsy Publications
Troy, OH 45373, U.S.A.
www.GypsyPublications.com

First Edition

Fisher, Meaghan
The Strawberry Festival
Story by Meaghan Fisher; Illustrated by Sandra Burns

ISBN 978-1-938768-60-6 (paperback)

Library of Congress Control Number
2015939513

Edited by Jon Williams
Book Design by Tim Rowe

To my darling children,
Emma Rose and Kevin, and to the
Strawberry Festival for all the
wonderful memories.

Kevin and Emma Rose were so excited. "Yay!" they cheered as Mama and Daddy walked to the downtown square. "The Strawberry Festival is here!"

The Strawberry Festival was held every year in June and it was every child's favorite time of year.

"I can't wait for strawberry doughnuts and strawberry pies!" shouted Kevin to his sister.

"Me too!" said Emma Rose as she twirled around in the pretty new strawberry dress Mama had just bought for the festival.

As they rounded the corner in the town's square, they saw that everyone was gathered for the Bed Races. The contestants were ready for the race to begin. Some had clown makeup on, and some had clown wigs, and others were dressed up like strawberries with big red smiles painted on their faces.

"They look silly, Mama!" Emma Rose giggled.

Suddenly, the announcer spoke and everyone gathered closer to the street and waited for the race to begin.

BANG! The race had begun! The silly racers pushed their beds around the square as fast as they could as their beds fell apart. Pillows hit the road and sheets flew around in the wind, with strawberry decorations flying everywhere. Some racers even fell off their beds as they ran.

Contestants hurried to gather up their things and stuff them back into their beds. They laughed as they pushed their beds down the street.

"They look so silly," said Kevin as he and his sister watched.

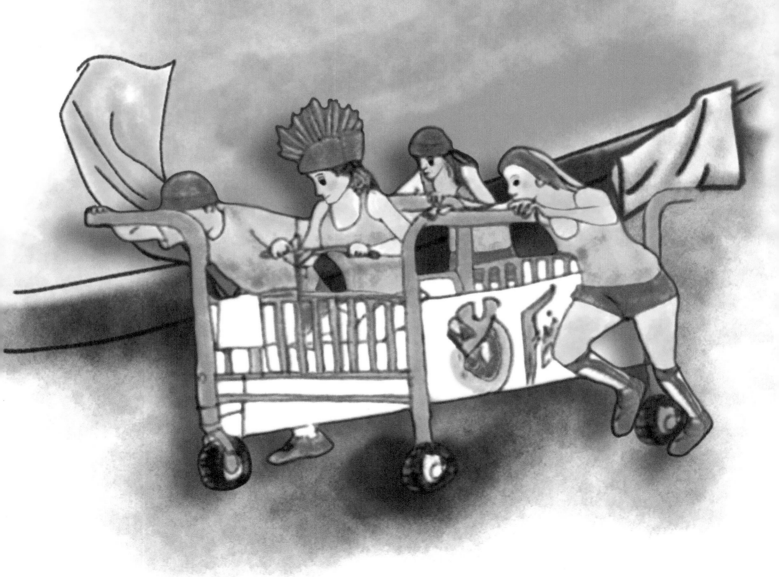

"Yes," said Mama. "But the whole point is to be silly and have fun! It's not important who wins. As long as you have fun doing it, that's all that matters!" Mama hugged her little ones as they watched the Bed Races end.

The next day was Saturday, the day of the big Strawberry Festival parade!

The kids walked into town with Mama and Daddy and picked a perfect grassy spot on Main Street. They couldn't wait to watch all the pretty floats go by and wave to all the people in the parade.

Mama and Daddy sat down on a blanket
with their two children and gave them each a
strawberry doughnut fresh from the festival.

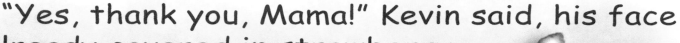

"Yum!" Emma Rose said as she had her first bite. "So good, Mama! Thank you!"

"Yes, thank you, Mama!" Kevin said, his face already covered in strawberry.

"You're welcome," replied Mama as she took pictures of her strawberry-covered kids. "Look! The parade is starting!"

Kevin and Emma Rose watched the High School Band march by, blowing their horns and crashing their cymbals.

They watched as Miss Strawberry and the Strawberry Queen Float went by with all the pretty girls on it looking like princesses, which was Emma Rose's favorite float!

They watched as the old cars carrying the Mayor and the County Commissioners went by, and they waved to all their friends and family they knew in the parade. But the best part came at the end!

MISS STRAWBERRY

STRAWBERRY
QUEEN

Kevin saw the fire truck coming down the street, with firemen waving and passing out candy to all the kids. He jumped to his feet to see the fire truck's driver. He had a big fireman's hat on, and beside him sat his spotted Dalmatian.

The fireman saw Kevin's excitement and threw him a big piece of candy. "Stay safe!" he called down to the kids.

"That was the best parade ever!" shouted Kevin as he unwrapped the candy the fireman had tossed to him. His parents smiled as they gathered up their things. It was time for the festival!

As the family arrived at the levee for the festival, the kids were so excited.

"Look at all the pretty things," said Emma Rose as she peeked into the vendors' tents, seeing all kinds of paintings and crafts for sale.

After they looked into all the tents they stopped to get strawberry lemonade. Then it was time to go play! As they walked down toward the river, they saw the dancing strawberries from the morning's parade.

"Hi, strawberries!" exclaimed Emma Rose and Kevin as they ran over and began dancing with them.

After dancing with the strawberries for a while, the
two children eagerly took off their shoes and into the
bouncy house they went! They leapt about as their
parents took pictures.

"I'm starving," said Daddy when the kids came out. "I think it's time for some pork chops and strawberry salsa! What do you think?"

"Yeah! Let's eat, Daddy!" shouted the kids.

A few minutes later, the family gathered up their food and walked along the levee, where they sat down to eat. The kids smiled as they ate the Strawberry Festival foods they loved best.

"Mama, this was the best Strawberry Festival ever!" Emma Rose said, giving her mother a big hug. "I can't wait to come again next year!"

CPSIA information can be obtained at www.ICGtesting.com
Printed in the USA
BVOW10s2244300815

415515BV00002B/3/P